THE FOLLIES OF FOSDICK

BY

HENRY CLAY MORRISON

First Fruits Press
Wilmore, Kentucky
c2013

ISBN: 9781621711292 (Print), 9781621711308 (Digital)

The Follies of Fosdick by Henry Clay Morrison
First Fruits Press, © 2013
Pentecostal Publishing Company, ©1936

Digital version at
http://place.asburyseminary.edu/firstfruitsheritagematerial/73/

Morrison, H. C. (Henry Clay), 1857-1942.
    The follies of Fosdick / by Henry Clay Morrison.
    45 p. ; 21 cm.
    Wilmore, Ky. : First Fruits Press, c2013.
    Reprint. Previously published: Louisville, Ky. : Pentecostal Pub. Co., c1936.
    ISBN: 9781621711292 (pbk.)
    1. Fosdick, Harry Emerson, 1878-1969. 2. Modernism (Christian theology) 3. Modernist-fundamentalist controversy. I. Title.
    BX6495.F68 M6 2013

Cover design by Haley Hill

asburyseminary.edu
800.2ASBURY
204 North Lexington Avenue
Wilmore, Kentucky 40390

First Fruits
THE ACADEMIC OPEN PRESS OF ASBURY SEMINARY

THE

FOLLIES

Of

FOSDICK

REV. H. C. MORRISON

❖ ❖ ❖

Pentecostal Publishing Co.
Louisville, Ky.

FOREWORD

We have never been able to find out what that class of preachers and teachers who are known as modernists believe. Their unbeliefs are more prominent than their beliefs. For instance, they do not believe the Mosaic record of the creation of the physical universe and of human beings. They do not believe that the prophets of the Old Testament Scriptures were divinely inspired, that they were able to look into the distant future and prognosticate with accuracy coming events.

They do not believe that Jesus Christ was pre-existent, that He was born of a virgin, that He was in a distinct and peculiar sense the Son of God, that He performed miracles, that His crucifixion in any way provided an atonement for the sinfulness of mankind. They do not believe in the physical resurrection of the body of Christ after His crucifixion and burial in Joseph's new tomb. They do not accept the New Testament teachings with reference to the deity and saving power of our Lord Jesus.

In a word, the modernists in our pulpits throughout the land in various churches reject the teachings of the

Scriptures concerning the Lord Jesus, His coming into the world to seek and to save the lost, and the blood atonement He made upon the cross for the sins of a fallen and lost race. The modernists have no gospel of hope with a promise of pardon to those who seek the forgiveness of their sins through the merit of a crucified and risen Christ.

Modernists do not believe in revivals of religion, occasions when the church is called together for the preaching of Christ to be received as a Savior through repentance and trust in Him as one able to save to the uttermost. They have no sympathy with the idea of a congregation of people who claim to have found salvation in the Lord Jesus setting special occasions to gather in the church for the Gospel message in sermon and song and earnest prayer, visitation, entreaty, and exhortation to the sinful to forsake their sins and come to Christ for forgiveness. Modernists, in their attitude and teaching, oppose every fundamental doctrine of our holy Christianity as contained in the Old and New Testaments. They have no sort of saving message for the individual sinner. They do not undertake to build upon any sort of scriptural foundation, a system of Gospel truth applicable to the needs of lost humanity. They cannot approach the deathbed of a dying sinner, however penitent such sinner may be, and point said sinner to Jesus Christ as one who is able and willing to forgive sin and bring peace and comfort into the distressed soul facing death and eternity without hope or consolation.

In the nature of things, modernists are engaged in destroying rather than in building. They constantly attack the Scriptures, the teachings of the prophets, Christ, and the apostles. They would take all the supernatural out of prophecy and the entire account of the virgin birth of Christ and the miracles He performed away from us. They would leave us practically nothing in the Old or New Testament upon which we could rest our faith for the forgiveness of our sins and our hope for peace and joy in the world to come.

The influence of these teachers is spreading through the church and the nation, paralyzing and destroying faith and opening wide the floodgates of unbelief of every sort. The fearful conditions in Russia, with its atheism, blasphemy, slaughter of the faithful, and tyranny over the souls and bodies of men, do not appear to frighten them or to stay their attacks upon inspired truth and the church of God. They seem to be blind and deaf to the loss of spiritual life, the destruction of moral standards, and the plague of unbelief and the fearful riot of sin in the nations of the world.

Shall those of us who believe in the inspiration of the Holy Scriptures, who by repentance and faith have found in Jesus Christ a personal Savior, whose divine power has transformed our lives, broken the power of sin, and brought us peace and joy—shall we be indifferent to this plague and paralysis of false teaching and unbelief. Shall there be no protest or tremendous effort to awaken the church to its danger and to bring about a counter-tide of spiritual truth and power to offset the destructive influence of their teachings? Can men of God, ministers and laity, be true to the Lord, themselves, the church, and the unsaved, and not give themselves with devout earnestness to contention for the faith?

CONTENTS

CHAPTER I

UNSCRIPTURAL TEACHINGS OF THE REV.
HARRY EMERSON FOSDICK

I have recently read with interest two of Dr. Fosdick's latest books: "As I See Religion." This book was published in 1932. His latest volume, "The Secret of Victorious Living," is a book of sermons published in 1934. These books are not without much interesting truth, most attractively presented.

Dr. Fosdick is a man of education, wide reading, much travel, and large opportunity for the gathering of information with reference to men and things in the world at large. He has a fascinating personality and is able to charm his audiences in the pulpit and that much wider hearing he has over the radio. He is easily one of the most popular radio preachers in the nation. He is evidently a man of genial spirit and kindly feeling toward those who are in sympathy with his very liberal religious views. He appears to greatly enjoy ridiculing those who cling tenaciously to the old faith in the inspiration of the Scriptures, the deity and saving power of our Lord Jesus Christ.

Many people are fascinated with the charming manner in which he presents his views, the wit and humor he employs in his defense of his position and attacks upon those who are disturbed and grieved with his assaults upon the foundations of the church of the Lord Jesus Christ. It has occurred to me to put before the readers of this booklet some of the teachings of this brilliant preacher which are entirely contrary to all evangelical Christianity. We could go through these books with many quotations, but we shall give only a few that are sufficient to show to the reader that if we are to accept the teachings of Dr. Fosdick and his school we must give up the Christian faith which through the centuries has rested firmly upon the divine inspiration of the Scriptures, the deity and saving power of our Lord Jesus Christ.

In the first chapter of the book on "As I See Religion," we find this statement: "All theology tentatively phrases in current thought and language the best that, up-to-date, thinkers on religion have achieved; and the most hopeful

thing about any system of theology is
that it will not last."

Evidently Dr. Fosdick does not believe that we have yet found an infalli-
ble foundation upon which to build a
system of divine truth that is trustworthy, that will abide, a Rock of Ages
on which we can rest our faith with a
full assurance of salvation, something
to be believed, preached, preserved, and
handed down from generation to generation, upon which men may build
their hopes for deliverance from sin and
everlasting life.

I recently asked one of our teachers
in the Theological Seminary at Asbury
College the simple question, What is
theology? He at once gave me this
answer:

"Christian theology has to do with
the existence and character of God, and
his relations to man, his purpose in the
creation of man, and his purpose in the
provision for his redemption and salvation here and his glory hereafter.

"It includes a careful study of man
and his moral nature, fall, sin and corruption, moral ruin and need; of salvation in atonement both for guilt and
corruption of sin under power of Pen-

tecostal grace as administered by the Holy Ghost.

"It recognizes and upholds the authority and integrity of the Holy Scriptures as the word of God for the purpose for which he intended them as Paul declared to Timothy in 2 Tim. 3:15-17.

"In this the meaning and glory of life and task from God appear and, under abounding grace, the call to faith and life and battle and holy triumph becomes clear and challenging.

"The true principles of righteousness and of righteous living are set forth both for the individual, and for the families and nations of earth."

This man is a graduate of one of the great universities of the nation and took his course in theology in Drew Seminary many years ago when it was supposed to be very free from any taint of modernism. He is a man who has traveled extensively in Europe and Palestine, always a close and scholarly student of men, books and things, who is well acquainted with the present-day trend of that modernism that is working havoc with the Christian faith of this nation.

A thoughtful study of the statement this professor gave me, I think, will convince any serious person that the content of this statement is accurate and sound, that it will do to build upon, that time will not wear it out, that it is abiding truth. There are some things in God's universe that are not ephemeral, that are not mere dreams and fancies, that will abide, that have stood the test of centuries and cannot pass away. The great facts of God, of sin, of redemption in Christ by repentance and faith, have stood the test of the centuries, have brought pardon, peace, and abiding hope to multiplied millions of people who have passed with joy to Paradise.

Good men have had some very crude notions about God and salvation which are unscriptural, some of which have passed away and others are on the road to the discard. Men have rebelled against the Calvinistic ideas once preached as inspired truth, that God fore-ordained and created certain human beings to be damned in a horrible hell through all eternity for His glory. There was a time when men believed this sort of thing with a sort of holy awe and there are those who cling to this false conception of God with grea tenacity. It is encouraging that they are getting a bit ashamed to affirm such things publicly.

The passing away of such false notions of God, so contrary to His nature and the revelation of His love and the gift of His Son, Jesus Christ, and the glad proclamation that He, by the grace of God, hath tasted death for every man, and that whosoever will may come and partake of the waters of life freely, will not and cannot pass away. God abides, Christ is the Rock of Ages that has stood the test of the centuries, has been, is and will be able to save all those who come to Him for forgiveness.

It is interesting and encouraging to note that Dr. Fosdick feels quite sure that his system of theology will not last. The sooner it passes the better, if he has any such thing as a systematic arrangement of divine truth. It is quite possible that this brilliant preacher does not really believe his own beliefs or rather his unbeliefs. Most modernists who attack the Scriptures and take delight in the ridicule of those who believe the same, have no definite Gospel message to offer the people. They seem to realize that their faiths are built upon the sand. They are constantly on the move. They have a sad lack of anything like permanency of faith or a positive message to deliver to a distressed world. "Other foundations can no man lay than that which is laid in Christ Jesus." Having rejected the Christ of the Scriptures, they are wanderers with no definite goal, no restful faith, no saving gospel.

CHAPTER II

From time immemorial, men have attacked the Bible, the deity and saving power of our Lord, and all the truths of a vital Gospel, which is the power of God unto salvation. This spirit of unbelief and opposition to divine truth is explained by the apostle when he wrote, "The carnal mind is enmity against God, is not subject to the law of God, neither indeed can be."

It is well understood that the penitent sinner does not need to understand creeds or to be an efficient student of theology in order to exercise saving faith in Christ. While this is true, the evangel which brings to the sinner the inspired truth that puts him under conviction and leads him to the exercise of saving faith in Christ, does need to have some sort of creed, whether it is in print upon paper or firmly fixed in his brain and heart.

There is such a thing as divine truth, something as eternal as God Himself, something that does not change, that,

like the Christ, is the same yesterday,
today, and forever. The safe religious
teacher should have some theologica'
knowledge, or, if you please, he ought
to have some definite idea of God, His
nature, His law, His love, and the terms
upon which He offers salvation. He
needs to know Jesus Christ as a sacrifice for sin, as a personal Savior. He
needs to know the Holy Spirit as a wit-
ness to his own heart of his salvation,
as a teacher, guide, comforter, and empowerer for service.

No man is prepared to preach the
Gospel who hasn't a knowledge of these
facts; very simple, perhaps, but very
clear in his personal consciousness. In
order to present the truth with any sort
of harmony, so that it will become ef-
fective in securing the end for which it
is and was designed, the preacher must
have some very definite knowledge, not
only of God and the plan of redemption,
but of sin and its effect upon men, and
its final fruitage and ruin.

The modernists are quite inclined to
have us toss overboard the Bible, Old
Testament and New, all creeds, and
theology, to discount everything in revealed and historic religion. They would

have us treat the past as if it were all blurred with ignorance, superstition, and hardly anything for which we should feel any reverence or promulgate as a saving and sanctifying influence. Meanwhile, it is quite noteworthy that they have nothing to offer us in the place of what the church has had in the past and now has.

Of course, we understand that mere creeds and a comprehensive knowledge of theology, do not save any one, but they contain revealed truth that if received and followed does lead the prodigal from the far country back to the Father's open arms of compassionate love. Our modernistic friends never major on the atonement made by Jesus Christ. They never with zeal and earnestness emphasize the importance of repentance and a look of faith to the Crucified One, with the assurance that they shall receive the forgiveness of their sins. Their business is to oppose and ridicule those who do hold steadfastly to the faith and preach the Gospel which has saved countless millions and transformed them from vilest sinners to happy saints.

We give a quotation from "As I See Religion," found on page 7, which reads: "We may have a religion toward which the preservative attitude prevails, as though our supreme concern were somehow to save it, or we may have a religion which we do not worry much about saving because it so vitally and visibly saves us." No doubt Dr. Fosdick regards that as a very brilliant and logical statement, and many of his shallow admirers will regard it as a religious and literary jewel.

But, thinking seriously, suppose we had found a religion that had brought to us a gracious pardon, a conscious transformation that had made us in Christ new creatures, will we not at once be interested in the salvation of others? And if we find modernistic pulpiteers attacking and ridiculing this religion that we have found so vital and so blessed, are we supposed to be unconcerned? Should we not naturally want to spread the religious truth that has brought us to Christ and a gracious assurance of salvation? And can we be indifferent to the attacks of those who would destroy both the Christ and the faith in Him which has brought us salvation? Thinking a moment, we find that the Doctor's reasoning is utterly shallow. It is not sound, spiritual sense, nor good religious literature. It's to trifle with sacred things. Blatant infi-dels have usually been willing for Christians to proclaim their faith and oppose those who would destroy their faith, but this man Fosdick has no such consideration of his brethren in the ministry. He constantly makes them the subject of ridicule.

Let me give you a further quotation on the same page: "Often with fever-ish militancy, always with deadly ear-nestness, they have made up their minds that religion must be saved. Such an attitude is a sure sign of religion's se-nility; it has uniformly preceded the downfall of those historic faiths that have grown old and passed away." There is quite a number of serious peo-ple that will not agree that the historic faiths have grown old and passed away. No doubt they have passed away in the mind of Dr. Fosdick. There are blind people who cannot see the sunshine at midday without a cloud, in the middle of August, but the sun is still shining.

What part of the old historic faith has passed away? Has the church abandoned belief in God, the Father, Christ, the Son, given as a holy sacrifice to save us from our sins, and the Holy Spirit as a comforter and empowerer? This faith was the foundation upon which the church of Jesus Christ was laid by the apostles and this faith abides. It has not passed away. These men who have given up the faith are constantly insisting that it is gone. They make many claims for young people and the rising generation, which are not true. These claims are made in order to deceive and influence young people and entice them to believe that the old faiths are dead and that we must let the modernist prepare some sort of a substitute for the religion revealed in the Holy Scriptures. The pure Gospel proclaimed by our Lord, John, Peter, and Paul, abides in the world and blesses the multitudes. The trouble with men like Dr. Fosdick is they hold no revivals, they do not see people under conviction for sin, seeking the Lord. They do not attend the hundreds of camp meetings held in this country, where multitudes of people seek pardon and mercy and sanctifying grace. They seem to think that the prison house of unbelief, in which they and their followers meet to destroy the faith of the people in the Bible, the virgin-born Christ, and His saving power, is all there is left in the world. Were this true, the church would be bankrupt indeed and Communism, with its blasphemy, blood, and tyranny, would take charge of the world. We quote from the same volume:

"While the early Christians battled stoutly for the things they believed, their major stress was not somehow to save their faith, anxiously defend it, and see it through. Their faith saved them, defended them, and saw them through. It carried them. It was to them health, peace, joy, and moral power. And whenever men thus have a religion which vitally saves them they have a religion which they need not worry much about saving."

It would seem impossible for a man of the intelligence of Dr. Fosdick, who is evidently well acquainted with the history of the early church, to write anything so entirely contrary to the facts. The men and women of the early church so earnestly believed in the Savior and the salvation which they had received through Him that they "anxiously defended it"—to the death. There was no earthly power to make them recant. They were saved by divine life and love that gave them the deepest concern for their fellowbeings that the Gospel truth which had brought them to Christ should abide and be proclaimed throughout the world, that they went to the stake by the thousands, they were fed to wild beasts. May I suggest to Dr. Fosdick and those who are so shallow in their thinking that they give any sort of credence to quotations like this above, that they read the eleventh chapter of the Epistle to the Hebrews. He and his school of thinkers will find that these early Christians were so eager to preserve the faith and hand it down to coming generations that they did not hesitate to suffer any privation, sacrifice, and even death itself to preserve the faith which they enjoyed from the opposition and bloody torture of those ancient modernists who had no more faith in the Bible and the Christ of the Bible and His saving Gospel than Dr. Fosdick and his fond and deluded followers.

CHAPTER III

We give the following quotation from the twenty-first page of "As I See Religion:"

"Moreover, when the modern mind hears the creeds upon which many of the churches still insist, with all the corollaries brought out by controversy and urged as indispensables of religious truth—old cosmologies, doctrines of biblical infallibility, miracles like virgin birth or physical resurrection—the reaction is not simply incredulity, although incredulity is undoubtedly emphatic—but wonder as to what such things have to do with religion."

The modernist liberalists have quite a bit to say of the modern mind. They seem to have an idea that the modern mind is quite superior, that the notions of most any skeptic are of more value to our times than the writings of the apostle Paul or the records of the New Testament. They might better say the modern skeptical mind cannot understand how a trustworthy Bible or the virgin birth of Christ or His physical resurrection and "such things have anything to do with religion." Notice the expression "SUCH THINGS." We would have been quite surprised if our skeptical Doctor had said, "such *facts*." With him, a divinely inspired Bible, the virgin birth of Christ, and His bodily resurrection, are just "such things" and belong to a realm of incredulity.

With the church of Christ, which is bringing salvation to a lost world, an inspired Bible, a virgin-born Christ, who arose from the dead and gave His disciples positive proof that He was the identical Christ whom they had known before the crucifixion, took pains to show them that He was not a spirit but of flesh and bone, ate before them. walked among them, and gave them the most positive proof that He had arisen from the dead—of course, all this is mere "things" with our brilliant Mr. Fosdick. I do not recall of having read from any infidel a more direct and trifling attack upon the foundations of our Christianity than this contained in the quotation we have just given.

With all that the brilliant Dr. Fosdick

has to say about the worry and anxiety of fundamentalists to take care of their religion, and with what he has to say in ridicule of the virgin birth, it is quite reasonable to suppose that had he been in Jerusalem at the trial of Christ, he would have been quite willing to stand up and say to those haters of our Lord, "Gentlemen, this man claims pre-existence and that he came down from his father in heaven. I cannot accept this statement. He appears to have performed miracles. I insist that it was some sort of sleight-of-hand performance. It is unthinkable that he ever performed miracles. I understand that he has said that he will rise from the dead. That is an impossibility and a fanatical boast." Undoubtedly had Dr. Fosdick lived in the days of our Lord and been present at His trial, with as little faith in the Christ as he now has, he would have joined with those who condemned Him as a pretender.

We quote the following from the book of sermons, "The Secret of Victorious Living:"

"I wonder if it is an accident that after the mountaintop communion of the

Master the Fourth Gospel says that, coming down, he walked upon the tempestuous waves of Galilee, and other Gospels add that the winds ceased. Many of you do not believe that such a thing really happened; no sea storm ever was so stopped, you say, nor did any one walk upon the water. *No more do I believe that it really happened,* but because we do not literally accept such miracle stories is no reason for regarding them as meaningless. They never will tell that kind of story about us, that we came down from a mountaintop communion so radiant with power that we walked the stormy waves and stilled the winds. Not even if we had lived in first-century Palestine, where such miracles were easily credited, would they ever have told that about us. But they did tell it about Jesus. Something happened in him on that mountaintop so that when he came down he seemed to his disciples to walk the world's tempests and quell them."

This quotation is quite interesting. Dr. Fosdick sweeps away this thrilling and miraculous manifestation of the Godhead which the Lord Jesus Christ gave of His power over the winds and waves of the sea. With the doubting Doctor, this, with all the miracles that took place at a time and in a country where such miracles were easily credited is swept away. My reader, suppose that we accept and follow after Fosdickism. However witty or brilliant or humorous this popular preacher may be, what would be some of the results. We would be bound to give little credit to the writings of Moses. We must tear out the prophecies of the Old Testament, so far as their containing any divine revelation which enabled them to correctly prognosticate the future. We must tear out the records of Matthew and Luke with reference to the virgin birth and the coming kingdom of Christ. We must tear out all the record of the miracles contained in the four Gospels. And what would we have left?

The situation in this country is much more serious than many easy-going people suppose. There is a tremendous drift in many ministers away from revealed truth to the skeptical teachings of the modern liberalists. If we follow

them and tear up the Scriptures as I
have suggested, have we not very clearly agreed with atheists and infidels?
Are we not in closer harmony with the
blasphemy and slaughter of Communism in Russia than we are with the historic church of Christ?   If this sort of
skepticism continues among popular
and handsomely paid preachers, and in
many of our seminaries, what are we to
expect in the not distant future?   Sat-
urate the present generation with these
false teachings, and what about the rising generation?   If we hand them down
no religious teaching that is emphatic,
no creed that we believe to be based upon divine truth, no theology that gives
proper interpretation of the divine be-
ing, sinful humanity, and the revealed
plan of salvation, but, having drifted
far from Bible truth, the apostles, the
prophets, and Christ the chief corner-
stone, what will the coming generations
have to believe or to save them from
blasphemous Communism?   How long
will it be until we have in this nation a
duplicate of conditions in Russia?

CHAPTER IV

THE DRIFT BECOMES A STRONG CURRENT

I might continue to quote from the two books that I have mentioned. Many paragraphs give us positive proof that Dr. Fosdick ought to get on very peaceably with the increasing number of atheists and skeptics who deny the inspiration of the Scriptures, the pre-existence, virgin birth, and blood atonement which Christ made for our sins, the resurrection of our Lord and the Gospel message which has been the power of God unto salvation through the centuries.

It is startling when we contemplate how many ministers in our pulpits and teachers in various seminaries have gone far more than half-way on the journey to outspoken and blasphemous skepticism. The fact is that many bold infidels who sneer at everything sacred are coming to claim the modernistic liberalists as their near kin. A soapbox skeptical orator not long since, referring to one of the very liberal preachers in the city where he was orating on the

streets, said, "The only difference between us is, I stand here and preach my
skepticism in the streets for nothing
while Dr. *Blank* (calling the preacher
by name) stands in his pulpit and
preaches to a people, claiming to be the
church of Christ, the same things that
I speak here, for a large salary paid
him by a people claiming to be the
church of Christ."

The soapbox orator brought from the
godless crowd about him cheers and
sneers and helped to kindle within their
breasts a spirit of hatred against the
church and all it is supposed to stand
for, while under the leadership of its
modernistic pastor, it is leading nobody
to Christ, destroying the faith, and not
only preparing the soil for the seed of
the skeptic but sowing the seed themselves, and, in fact, was a far more dan-
gerous man to the church and society
than the blasphemous man on the soapbox in the street.

We quote the following from page
163 of "As I See Religion:"

"Undoubtedly, however, the whole
idea of supernatural dictation has pe-
tered out. 'Thou shalt not commit

adultery' seems to many of us excellent morals. This generation, however, will walk around the idea, look it over, size it up, watch its consequences, listen to any one from Bertrand Russell to Bishop Manning, and decide; but one thing this generation will not do is to accept even that command on supernatural authority."

This is a rather startling paragraph. Are we to understand that Dr. Fosdick has made a surrender of the Holy Scriptures? Does he mean to tell us that this generation has no more reverence for the Ten Commandments, that the young people growing up about us have no sort of faith in a supernatural authority, that they have discarded God, blasphemed the Holy Ghost, and are quite indifferent to that commandment, "Thou shalt not commit adultery?" It would seem that the dear man proposes a surrender or has reached the conclusion that the present young generation has gone so far away from the faith of the fathers that they are utterly indifferent to any such thing as supernatural, that is, divine authority, that is, reverence or an attitude of obedience toward God.

We should have a bit of patience toward Dr. Fosdick. He lives in the great modern Sodom of the world, New York City, with its mingled multitudes from the various nations of the earth, with its millionaires on one hand and its extreme poverty on the other, with corrupt politics, with powerful combinations of vice for the blighting of the young, its traffic in white slavery, its vulgar shows and carnal pastimes, its skepticism in pulpit and unbelief in pews, without any sort of evangelism in his own church surrounded and flattered by a people who reject the Christ of prophecy and the New Testament. He is quite liable to mistake the attitude of the rising generation and conclude that because he has lost faith in the supernatural an entire generation has utterly abandoned and cast away the Bible with its Ten Commandments, its Sermon on the Mount, the wonderful record of the miracles and the glorious atonement that our triumphant and resurrected Lord made for us upon the cross of Calvary.

It is my privilege to be in close touch

as an evangelist and editor, along with
the presidency of a college, with vast
numbers of young people.   I preach to
them, meet them face to face, corre-
spond with them, and I know beyond
question or doubt that we have in the
rising generation vast multitudes of
young people who do believe in the supernatural.   They believe the Ten Commandments are of divine authority.
They do not believe that they are tyran-
nical or whimsical.   They believe all of
the "shalt nots" contained in the Ten
Commandments would warn us against
going over the abyss of ruin.   They believe that the "thou shalts" of the Commandments are stepladders upon which
we may climb to pluck the fruits of
peace and righteousness.

One of the troubles with your modern
liberalists is they are constantly prophe-
sying conditions that they desire to
have exist.   They want the young people of the rising generation to give up
historic Christianity and follow their
deceptive teachings into the wide wild-
erness of know-nothingism, no positive
faith in Christ as a divine and risen
Lord able to save from sin.   All the

beautiful sayings of the Doctor about experimental religion fall to pieces and are without meaning when he gives up Jesus Christ as the only name among men by which we may be saved. We must keep Jesus in the midst. He and He alone can save. And when we discard Him we are not only lost but we have re-crucified the Son of God, put Him to an open shame, and made our own salvation an impossibility.

CHAPTER V

THE SUPREMACY OF CHRIST

It has been quite customary for men who reject the Godhead and saving power of Jesus Christ to say very beautiful things about His character and teaching. This is not enough. Jesus Christ must be recognized as the Son of God in that high and holy sense which He claims for Himself, reverenced as such, sought and trusted in as a Savior from sin, if we would meet the requirements of the Holy Scriptures and find in Him both Savior and Lord. Nothing short of this will meet the obligations which divine truth lays upon us. Compliments of His beautiful character and splendid teachings are not enough. By faith, He may and must become a personal Savior.

Lecky, the historian, who was a rationalist, says of Jesus: "In the character and example of Christ, there is an enduring principle of regeneration." Evidently, this writer was not thinking of the new birth of the individual, but more broadly of the regeneration or the uplift and elevation of human society. If all men carefully practiced the teachings of Christ and sought to pattern after Him in the development of character, it would transform society. Wars would cease. The liquor traffic would pass away. And we would have an entirely different civilization. But somehow that sort of thing does not work. Men are naturally sinful and selfish. The individual must be regenerated, born again, become in Christ a new creature. If we ever bring into the nations of the earth peace and harmony, it must be by bringing the individual units into that new life that can only be received by faith in Christ as Savior.

Renan, an infidel, says, "The person of Jesus is the highest summit of human greatness." This is doubtless true. Jesus was at the summit of human greatness, but He was far more than this. He was not only human, but He was divine. He was man enough to sympathize with us and God enough to save us. A high priest who could be touched with the feeling of our infirmities that He might sympathize with us, a divine Christ that, through the

atonement on the cross, He might forgive our transgressions and cleanse us
from all sin.

John Stuart Mill, philosopher and
agnostic, says of Jesus, "Everything
which is excellent in ethics may be
brought within the sayings of Christ,
without doing violence to the language.
He is the ideal representative and guide
to humanity." This is a very high tribute to our Lord and His teachings,
which cover the whole realm of human
ethics,—the relation between husband
and wife, parents and children, capital
and labor, men and their fellowbeings
everywhere.

If Jesus was all these skeptical philosophers claim for Him, He was far
more than what they claim. It must be
remembered that Jesus speaks for Himself. If what He said of Himself was
not true, He was the greatest pretender
and false teacher that ever appeared
among men. If these philosophers
whom I have quoted spoke the truth, it
is quite impossible that He was a pretender and false teacher. He was all He
claimed for Himself.

You remember that in John 17:4, 5,

Jesus very clearly claims pre-existence.
We read: "I have glorified thee on the
earth. I have finished the work which
thou gavest me to do. And now, O father, glorify thou me with thine own self
with the glory which I had with thee before the world was." This is a very
clear statement made by our Lord Himself with reference to his pre-existence.
You will remember that Jesus on one
occasion said to those who contended
against Him, "I am before Abraham
was." Here is another claim to pre-existence. He did not hesitate to say, "I
came down from the Father."

Our Lord could have made no higher
claim for Himself than when He said,
"I am the way, the truth, and the life."
And again, we hear Him saying, "I am
the resurrection and the life." And
again, "I am the door." And again,
"No man knoweth the Father save
the Son and he to whom the Son re-
veals him." Jesus Christ received worship; when He healed the ten lepers and
one returned and fell at his feet wor-
shipping Him He did not rebuke him,
but said, "Were there not ten cleansed?
Where are the nine?" Our Lord Jesus

invited all men with their burdens and sorrows to come to Him with the promise that He would give them rest. He repeatedly claimed the power and authority to forgive sin. He assured in a number of instances that He would return to this globe in great glory and power. If these claims of the Lord Jesus were false, no man has a right to pay to Him the high tributes quoted in this chapter.

Finally, we shall have to accept Jesus on the basis of his own statement with reference to Himself or we will not only have to reject Him but what these philosophers and various and sundry modern liberalists have to say of His beautiful character and the excellence of His teachings.

The inspired writers claimed for Jesus infinitely more than philosophers and modernists who reject His Godhead and at the same time would pay him a high tribute of praise. St. John tells us that "in the beginning was the Word, and the Word was with God, and the Word was God. The same was in the beginning with God. All things were made by him, and without him was not anything made that was made. In him was life; and the life was the light of men. And the light shineth in darkness; and the darkness comprehendeth it not." And there's the rub. The darkened minds of men refuse to receive the Christ and trust in Him as a Savior. Those who have accepted Him, as described to us by John in these gracious verses of the first chapter of his Gospel, have found Him to be all John claims for Him.

St. Paul exalts Jesus Christ high above all men and angels. We read in Hebrews, the first chapter: "For unto which of the angels said he at any time, Thou art my Son, this day have I begotten thee? And again, I will be to him a Father, and he shall be to me a Son? And again, when he bringeth in the firstbegotten into the world, he saith, And let all the angels of God worship him. And of the angels he saith, Who maketh his angels spirits, and his ministers a flame of fire. But unto the Son he saith, Thy throne, O God, is for ever and ever: a sceptre of righteousness is the sceptre of thy kingdom."

It is sadly true that we are living in

an age of doubt. There has been a tremendous drift in the church toward a worldliness and unbelief that has sadly paralyzed spiritual power and evangelistic zeal. There is a spirit of arrogance and irreverence in the world that lends itself not only readily but eagerly to the false teaching of modernists, in pulpit and school, which is most destructive not only to spiritual life but to morals and everything that is good, decent, and for the best in human society. But in spite of all this, there are millions of people on earth who rest their faith for salvation in their crucified and risen Lord and go forward with a holy courage, believing and laboring until "His enemies be made his footstool."

"Rock of ages, cleft for me,
Let me hide myself in thee;
Let the water and the blood,
From thy wounded side which flowed,
Be of sin the double cure,
Save from wrath and make me pure."